My favorite Recipes book

Name
Mail
Mobile
Address

This book is copyright by @Vanessa Robins
June 2018

Recipe_____

Ingredients	Sources

Directions (How to cook)

Recipe_____

Ingredients	Sources

Directions (How to cook)

Recipe_____

Ingredients	Sources

Directions (How to cook)

Recipe_____

Ingredients	Sources

Directions (How to cook)

Recipe_____

Ingredients	Sources

Directions (How to cook)

Recipe_____

Ingredients	Sources

Directions (How to cook)

Recipe_____

Ingredients	Sources

Directions (How to cook)

Recipe_____

Ingredients	Sources

Directions (How to cook)

Recipe_____

Ingredients	Sources

Directions (How to cook)

Recipe_____

Ingredients	Sources

Directions (How to cook)

Recipe_____

Ingredients	Sources

Directions (How to cook)

Recipe_____

Ingredients	Sources

Directions (How to cook)

Recipe_____

Ingredients	Sources

Directions (How to cook)

Recipe_____

Ingredients	Sources

Directions (How to cook)

Recipe_____

Ingredients	Sources

Directions (How to cook)

Recipe_____

Ingredients	Sources

Directions (How to cook)

Recipe_____

Ingredients	Sources

Directions (How to cook)

Recipe_____

Ingredients	Sources

Directions (How to cook)

Recipe_____

Ingredients	Sources

Directions (How to cook)

Recipe_____

Ingredients	Sources

Directions (How to cook)

Recipe_____

Ingredients	Sources

Directions (How to cook)

Recipe_____

Ingredients	Sources

Directions (How to cook)

Recipe_____

Ingredients	Sources

Directions (How to cook)

Recipe_____

Ingredients	Sources

Directions (How to cook)

Recipe_____

Ingredients	Sources

Directions (How to cook)

Recipe_____

Ingredients	Sources

Directions (How to cook)

Recipe_____

Ingredients	Sources

Directions (How to cook)

Recipe_____

Ingredients	Sources

Directions (How to cook)

Recipe_____

Ingredients	Sources

Directions (How to cook)

Recipe_____

Ingredients	Sources

Directions (How to cook)

Recipe_____

Ingredients	Sources

Directions (How to cook)

Recipe_____

Ingredients	Sources

Directions (How to cook)

Recipe_____

Ingredients	Sources

Directions (How to cook)

Recipe_____

Ingredients	Sources

Directions (How to cook)

Recipe_____

Ingredients	Sources

Directions (How to cook)

Recipe_____

Ingredients	Sources

Directions (How to cook)

Recipe_____

Ingredients	Sources

Directions (How to cook)

Recipe_____

Ingredients	Sources

Directions (How to cook)

Recipe_____

Ingredients	Sources

Directions (How to cook)

Recipe_____

Ingredients	Sources

Directions (How to cook)

Recipe_____

Ingredients	Sources

Directions (How to cook)

Recipe_____

Ingredients	Sources

Directions (How to cook)

Recipe_____

Ingredients	Sources

Directions (How to cook)

Recipe_____

Ingredients	Sources

Directions (How to cook)

Recipe_____

Ingredients	Sources

Directions (How to cook)

Recipe_____

Ingredients	Sources

Directions (How to cook)

Recipe_____

Ingredients	Sources

Directions (How to cook)

Recipe_____

Ingredients	Sources

Directions (How to cook)

Recipe_____

Ingredients	Sources

Directions (How to cook)

Recipe_____

Ingredients	Sources

Directions (How to cook)

Recipe_____

Ingredients	Sources

Directions (How to cook)

Recipe_____

Ingredients	Sources

Directions (How to cook)

Recipe_____

Ingredients	Sources

Directions (How to cook)

Recipe_____

Ingredients	Sources

Directions (How to cook)

Recipe_____

Ingredients	Sources

Directions (How to cook)

Recipe_____

Ingredients	Sources

Directions (How to cook)

Recipe_____

Ingredients	Sources

Directions (How to cook)

Recipe_____

Ingredients	Sources

Directions (How to cook)

Recipe_____

Ingredients	Sources

Directions (How to cook)

Recipe_____

Ingredients	Sources

Directions (How to cook)

Recipe_____

Ingredients	Sources

Directions (How to cook)

Recipe_____

Ingredients	Sources

Directions (How to cook)

Recipe_____

Ingredients	Sources

Directions (How to cook)

Recipe_____

Ingredients	Sources

Directions (How to cook)

Recipe_____

Ingredients	Sources

Directions (How to cook)

Recipe_____

Ingredients	Sources

Directions (How to cook)

Recipe_____

Ingredients	Sources

Directions (How to cook)

Recipe_____

Ingredients	Sources

Directions (How to cook)

Recipe_____

Ingredients	Sources

Directions (How to cook)

Recipe_____

Ingredients	Sources

Directions (How to cook)

Recipe_____

Ingredients	Sources

Directions (How to cook)

Recipe_____

Ingredients	Sources

Directions (How to cook)

Recipe_____

Ingredients	Sources

Directions (How to cook)

Recipe_____

Ingredients	Sources

Directions (How to cook)

Recipe_____

Ingredients	Sources

Directions (How to cook)

Recipe_____

Ingredients	Sources

Directions (How to cook)

Recipe_____

Ingredients	Sources

Directions (How to cook)

Recipe_____

Ingredients	Sources

Directions (How to cook)

Recipe_____

Ingredients	Sources

Directions (How to cook)

Recipe_____

Ingredients	Sources

Directions (How to cook)

Recipe_____

Ingredients	Sources

Directions (How to cook)

Recipe_____

Ingredients	Sources

Directions (How to cook)

Recipe_____

Ingredients	Sources

Directions (How to cook)

Recipe_____

Ingredients	Sources

Directions (How to cook)

Recipe_____

Ingredients	Sources

Directions (How to cook)

Recipe_____

Ingredients	Sources

Directions (How to cook)

Recipe_____

Ingredients	Sources

Directions (How to cook)

Recipe_____

Ingredients	Sources

Directions (How to cook)

Recipe_____

Ingredients	Sources

Directions (How to cook)

Recipe_____

Ingredients	Sources

Directions (How to cook)

Recipe_____

Ingredients	Sources

Directions (How to cook)

Recipe_____

Ingredients	Sources

Directions (How to cook)

Recipe_____

Ingredients	Sources

Directions (How to cook)

Recipe_____

Ingredients	Sources

Directions (How to cook)

Recipe _____

Ingredients	Sources

Directions (How to cook)

Recipe_____

Ingredients	Sources

Directions (How to cook)

Recipe_____

Ingredients	Sources

Directions (How to cook)

Recipe_____

Ingredients	Sources

Directions (How to cook)

Recipe_____

Ingredients	Sources

Directions (How to cook)

Recipe_____

Ingredients	Sources

Directions (How to cook)

Recipe_____

Ingredients	Sources

Directions (How to cook)

Recipe_____

Ingredients	Sources

Directions (How to cook)

Recipe_____

Ingredients	Sources

Directions (How to cook)

Recipe_____

Ingredients	Sources

Directions (How to cook)

Recipe_____

Ingredients	Sources

Directions (How to cook)

Recipe_____

Ingredients	Sources

Directions (How to cook)

Recipe_____

Ingredients	Sources

Directions (How to cook)

Recipe_____

Ingredients	Sources

Directions (How to cook)

Recipe_____

Ingredients	Sources

Directions (How to cook)

Recipe_____

Ingredients	Sources

Directions (How to cook)

Recipe_____

Ingredients	Sources

Directions (How to cook)

Recipe_____

Ingredients	Sources

Directions (How to cook)

Made in the USA
Columbia, SC
22 June 2019